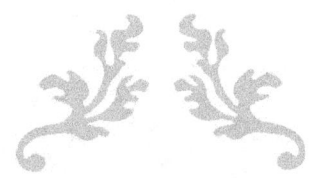

LET'S DRAW WITH RAY

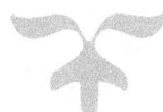

BY

THE BLACK HAITIAN BARBIE

Let's draw a <u>Jellyfish</u> with Ray.

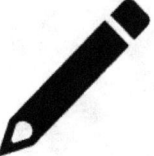

Let's draw a <u>Monkey</u> with Ray.

Let's draw a <u>Dog</u> with Ray.

Let's draw a <u>Cat</u> with Ray.

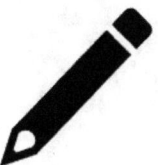

Let's draw a <u>Fish</u> with Ray.

Let's draw a <u>Lion</u> with Ray.

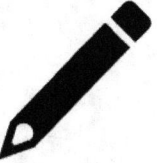

Let's draw a <u>Zebra</u> with Ray.

Let's draw a <u>Giraffe</u> with Ray.

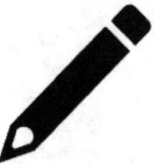

Let's draw a <u>Duck</u> with Ray.

Let's draw a <u>Flamingo</u> with Ray.

Let's draw a <u>Butterfly</u> with Ray.

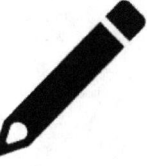

Let's draw a <u>House</u> with Ray.

Let's draw a <u>Tree</u> with Ray.

Draw a picture of <u>Your Family</u> with Ray.

Let's draw <u>Apples</u> with Ray.

Let's draw <u>Oranges</u> with Ray.

Let's draw <u>Cars</u> with Ray.

Let's draw <u>trucks</u> with Ray.

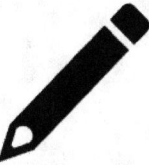

Let's draw <u>Flowers</u> with Ray.

Let's draw <u>Hearts</u> with Ray.

Let's draw <u>Stars</u> with Ray.

I left extra pages for you to draw on.

Thank you for drawing with me.

I am Ray.

I live in Orlando Florida

www.ingramcontent.com/pod-product-compliance
Lightning Source LLC
Chambersburg PA
CBHW081645220526
45468CB00009B/2559